**ANTI-SOCIAL CLIMBERS**

SIT DOWN! SIT DOWN! I HAVE A TREAT FOR YOU!

YAHOO!

ZOOM

WHEEE

WE'RE GOING TO HAVE A VISIT AND TALK FROM MISTER ROCK FACE, EXPLORER AND MOUNTAIN CLIMBER!

MR ROCK FACE

HA-HA!

DO ANY OF YOU HAVE ANY QUESTIONS FOR MISTER FACE?

YES! HOW DO YOU KEEP FROM FALLING ON ICY MOUNTAINS?

EASY! I USE THESE SPIKES. THEY CLIP ON TO YOUR BOOTS FOR EXTRA GRIP.

Suddenly —

YAHOO! WE'LL GIVE THEM A TRY.

STAMPEDE

BUMP

WAA!

And —

GREAT FOR CLIMBING WALLS, TOO, ROCK!

COME DOWN AT ONCE!

Then —

AND THE GOOD NEWS IS THAT YOU'RE GOING TO JOIN HIM, TEACHER!

EH? NO . . . WAIT! STOP!

PULL

EASY!

WHIMPER!

HAVING FUN, SIR?

Then —

HERE'S A CAKE FOR YOU, ROCK. BAKED BY OLIVE!

NO! DON'T TAKE IT! STOP!

YIKES! IT'S SO HEAVY!

WHEEE

OOOH!

FALL

SCHOOL NEWS CAPER

In class.

A QUESTION! WHAT IS THIS?

HMM! ER!

SHAKE

ER . . .

IT'S OUR SCHOOL MAGAZINE. IT'S EMPTY BECAUSE WE NEVER WIN ANYTHING TO WRITE ABOUT OR HAVE ANYTHING TO REPORT.

BASH STREET SCHOOL MAGAZINE

THAT'S WHY I'D LIKE YOU AL TO BE REPORTERS TODAY. G AND FIND A FEW GOOD STORIES FOR OUR MAGAZIN!

WAHEY! WE SURE WILL, SIR!

WAH! OOH!

WOW! IT'S TRUE!

ZOOM

SORRY! MY SIGN DROPPED OFF ITS HOOKS AGAIN.

FISH SHOP

AW! NOT A REAL STORY AFTER ALL.

PHEW!

LOOK! WHAT STORY THIS TIME.

AHA! CAN WE ASK YOU A FEW QUESTIONS, SIR?

ELLE

JEWELL

ER . . . I WAS GOING TO SWAT A FLY ON THE JEWELLER'S WINDOW WITH MY BRICK! THAT'S ALL — HONEST! I . . .

WHAT'S YOUR NAME? DO YOU LIVE IN BEANOTOWN?

WHAT JOB DO YOU HAVE?

AHA!

JEW

WELL DONE, KIDS! YOU'V CAUGHT 'SMASHER SMITH' THE INFAMOUS THIEF.

TAP! TAP!

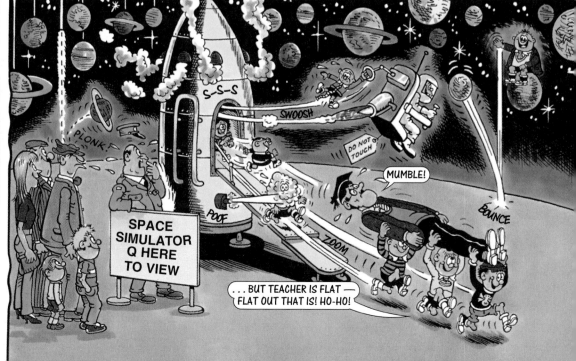

CLOTHES ENCOUNTERS

One morning —

WAHEY!

CRASH! RUMBLE

IIB

But —

WHERE'S TEACHER?

Then —

TAKE THESE WATER PISTOLS TO TEST THE SUITS!

GLUB!

SPLAT!

SPLOOSH!

Soon —

VERY GOOD! SUITS ARE SHRINK PROOF!

Next —

YUM!

FOR YOU, FATTY!

EXTRA HOT CURRY

HEH-HEH! A LOOK FROM PLUG'S FACE LIKE THAT WOULD MAKE NORMAL CLOTHES DISINTEGRATE!

IIB

OOOBLE! GROOO!

TWIST PULL

BUT THE SUITS SURVIVED! THANK YOU, PLUG!

So —

I'LL MAKE A FORTU WITH THESE SUITS! STREET KIDS PROOF EVERYONE WILL W THEM! YAHOO!

DA

LEAP

# JEST THE JOB

DO ANY OF YOU HAVE ANY IDEAS OF WHAT TYPE OF JOBS YOU'D LIKE TO DO ONCE YOU'VE LEFT BASH ST.? IF SO, HOW ABOUT SOME "WORK ROLL-PLAY ACTING"? ACT OUT THE JOB YOU'D LIKE TO DO HERE IN CLASS!

HMM!

RAZZZ!

OKAY!

WHO'D LIKE TO BE FIRST?

ME, SIR! I'D LIKE TO BE A BANK MANAGER!

SID A TOOT

YOU'D LIKE TO BE A TV WEATHERMAN?

YES!

RAIN

. . . WET HERE AND DRY OVER THE REST OF THE COUNTRY . . .

HUMPH!

HA-HA! HE'S MISSED THE CHART!

SUN RAIN SUN SNOW RAIN SNOW SUN

Next —

I'M GOING SHOPPING!

PUSH

TAKE A SEAT, TEACHER!

PLAYING ALONG ↓

HO-HO! YES, SIR!

YOUR TEACHING RECORD'S A DISGRACE!

EH . . . ?

TEACHER'S REPORT

PUPILS RUN WILD . . . DON'T DO HOMEWORK!

. . . WELL . . .

I CAN ONLY SEE ONE ANSWER . . . YOU'RE FIRED!

... MAY WE HAVE A VORD, MISTER BANK MANAGER?

YES ... DO COME IN. TAKE A SEAT, MR AND MRS SMITH!

WELL, WE'VE SPENT ALL OF OUR MONEY, ALL OF THE BANK'S MONEY AND WE'RE NOT GOING TO PAY YOU BACK!

HMMM! WELL ...

... YOU DESERVE A GOOD THUMPING!

LEAP

KICK

KICK

Bank

BIFF

SIGH! SOME BANK MANAGER!

BURP! SHOP'S CLOSED — WAITING FOR NEW STOCK! BOIYLP!

FATTY'S SHOP

CHOCOLATE   TOFFEE

CAKES   GATEAU

SIGH! A BAD CHOICE FOR FATTY — A SHOP KEEPER!

Then —

WOW!

SIT DOWN! STOP ALL OF THIS NONSENSE AT ONCE!

HO-HO! PLUG WANTS TO BE A SCHOOL HEADMASTER!

CHORTLE!

ME? FIRED? SIR!

SIGH! SACKED! HOW CAN I TELL MRS TEACHER?

OUT!

YAHOO! WELL DONE, PLUG!

TEACHER REALLY GOT INTO THE ROLL PLAYING GAME!

BY THE TIME IT DAWNS ON HIM THAT HE ISN'T SACKED ... IT'LL BE TOO LATE TO COME BACK TO SCHOOL FOR THE DAY!

BLAT

BOING

DONK

KICK

# UNHAPPY ANNIVERSARY

One morning —

SCHOOL PHOTO

GIBBER! WHAT'LL I DO... WHAT'LL I DO...

CHEW BITE

OO... WHAT'LL I D
I WAS MEANT TO TA
MRS TEACHER OUT
A MEAL FOR OUR WED
ANNIVERSARY — BU
FORGOT TO BOOK A TA

TEACHER LOOKS WORRIED AND WE HAVEN'T EVEN SAT DOWN YET!

Then —

This iz not a School

La Posh

TARA! NICE, EH?

HMM!

DUST COVER

RETURN TO SCHOOL THEATRE GROUP

NOT MANY PEOPLE HERE.

ER... MUST BE TOO EXPENSIVE FOR THEM, MY DEAR.

AHEM! GOOD EVENING, SIR!

Soon —

FISH AND CHIPS.

PROP

ENJOY YOUR MEAL!

SCREECH! WAIL!

MUSIC?

SCREECH! WAIL!

LISTEN, I'LL SNEAK OUT AND USE MY CAR TO GO TO THE CHINESE TAKEAWAY!

GOOD IDEA!

I'LL NOT BE LONG!

CLIMB

HELLO, HELLO, HELLO!

SO! A BURGLAR, EH?

CAUGHT YOU RED-HANDED!

GRAB

OO... NO!

HEH-HEH!

PROBLEM SOLVED! BRING MRS TEACHER BACK HERE ONCE THE SCHOOL IS CLOSED.

OO . . . ER!

WE CAN DISGUISE THE ROOM AND OURSELVES WITH PROPS FROM THE SCHOOL THEATRE STORE.

Later, after school —

PUT ON YOUR BEST FROCK, MRS TEACHER! WE'RE GOING OUT FOR AN ANNIVERSARY MEAL!

Shortly —

KEEP THE BLINDFOLD ON — I WANT IT TO BE A SURPRISE!

UMPH! ING FOR A ALREADY!

In the school kitchen —

WHAT CAN WE GIVE THEM TO EAT?

LEFT-OVERS

Then —

AHA! PLENTY OF GRUB HERE!

HOI!

FISH

CHIPS

GRAB

ER . . .

SCREECH!

SCREECH! WAIL! SCREECH! WAIL!

. . . OOW! STOP!

CHOMP! GOBBLE! MUNCH!

HOI! WHERE'D OUR GRUB GO?

HAR-HAR! NICE KEBAB!

The kids tell Mrs Teacher the whole story.

. . . SO WE WERE JUST TRYING TO HELP!

UMPH

BUT WE'VE LANDED TEACHER IN JAIL FOR THE NIGHT.

But —

WAHEY! BEST ANNIVERSARY PRESENT EVER! TEACHER LOCKED UP FOR THE NIGHT! I CAN GO HOME AND WATCH THE TELLY IN PEACE — WITHOUT TEACHER'S MOANING!

HA-HA!

LEAP

CHORTLE!

CLOCK BOTCHERS

In the Head's study.

BAH! SOMEONE'S BEEN SNAFFLING MY CHOCOLATE CHIP COOKIES AGAIN!

IT WASN'T US, HEAD . . . CRUNCH . . . HONEST . . .

ERM . . . WHY AMN'T I CONVINCED?

I NEED TO RECRUIT SOME ABLE SPRING CLEANERS, TEACHER.

I'LL LEAD YOU TO SOME WILLING HELPERS, OH NOBLE ONE!

BE GENTLE WITH MY FAMILY HEIRLOOMS, PUPILS.

GOSH! THERE'S ALL SORTS OF JUNK UP HERE.

THIS OLD HARP MAKE A SUPER CATAPULT!

TWANG

OOF!

THUD!

UNHAND THAT ANCIENT STRINGED INSTRUMENT, BOY!

Next —

HOI! DON'T TURN THAT HANDLE, 'ERBERT! OOH!

HA-HA! A GREAT IMPROVEMENT, PLUG!

SWEEP

THE HEAD WILL GO DING-DONG WHEN HE SEES THE STATE OF HIS CLOCK.

WE'LL STICK IT TOGETHER WITH CHEWING GUM — GET CLEANING!

CHEW! A FEW BITS OF GUM HERE AND A FEW BITS THERE.

TUG

STICK

LEFT-OVERS →

In the Head's study.

ALMOST AS GOOD AS NEW. NOW IN YOU GO, PLUG, AND DON'T FORGET TO CHIME ON THE HOUR.

BAH! I HAVE TO TURN THE CLOCK HANDS TOO.

HEAD'S WANTING VOLUNTEERS TO HELP CLEAN AND TIDY HIS ATTIC TODAY.

NO WAY!

CHOMP!

PUPILS WHO REFUSE TO HELP WILL COPY OUT THE COMPLETE WORKS OF SHAKESPEARE, BACKWARDS!

I'LL GET THE BRUSHES.

I'LL FETCH THE DUSTERS AND POLISH, SIR!

WELCOME TO MY MODEST HOME.

HO-HO! THE HEAD'S GARDEN GNOMES ALL LOOK LIKE TEACHER.

In the attic.

I HAVEN'T BEEN UP HERE SINCE BASH STREET SCHOOL LAST WON A TROPHY.

WELL, THAT MUST BE 40 OR 50 YEARS AGO!

JOLLY GOOD SHOW, CHAPS! NOW TAKE THIS BEAUTIFUL CLOCK TO MY STUDY.

OKAY!

DROP IT GENTLY!

THIS WAY!

THIS IS A GREAT WAY TO MOVE THE GRANDFATHER CLOCK!

ZOOM

But —

ER . . . WHAT WAS THAT NOISE?

CRASH

ZOOM

CRASH

BOING

DOING

ER . . . THE CLOCK!

BASH STREET SCHOOL

H, YES! THE CLOCK OKS SPLENDID. EH? HAT'S A STRANGE NOISE.

DING-DONG-ACHOO!

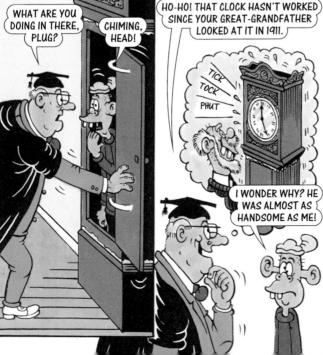

WHAT ARE YOU DOING IN THERE, PLUG?

CHIMING, HEAD!

HO-HO! THAT CLOCK HASN'T WORKED SINCE YOUR GREAT-GRANDFATHER LOOKED AT IT IN 1911.

TICK TOCK PHUT

I WONDER WHY? HE WAS ALMOST AS HANDSOME AS ME!

I'M USING IT AS A PLACE TO HIDE MY BICCIES FROM TEACHER AND THE JANITOR.

PLOP

BICCIES

BICCIES

CRUNCH

MUNCH

HA-HA! MUM'S THE WORD, HEAD!

# WHAT GOES ON BEHIND THE BIKE SHED

HUH? BUT WE ALWAYS SKIVE BEHIND THE BIKE SHED.

KEEP OUT

GO AWAY

NO ADMITTANCE

LOOKS LIKE A SIGN.

HMM! SOMEBODY'S TRYING TO TELL US SOMETHING.

WHAT'S GOING ON ROUND THERE?

TWEAK!
SCREW!
TWIDDLE-TAP!

KEEP OUT

NO ADMIT

AND ROUND THERE IS OUR TERRITORY.

ALL FINISHED, SIR. JUST THE WAY YOU WANTED.

EXCELLENT, JANITOR!

KEEP

EH?

GO

FOLLOW ME, AND NO PEEPING. I'VE A SURPRISE FOR YOU.

COR! WE LIKE SURPRISES.

CAN'T WAIT TO SEE IT.

NO ADD

WAHEY! IT'S A BICYCLE MADE SPECIALLY FOR US BASH STREET KIDS.

NOW I CAN KEEP AN EYE ON THEM ALL AT THE SAME TIME.

GO AWAY

KEEP OUT

WE'VE GOT PEDAL POWER!

CRUNCH!

COR! YOU COULDN'T FIT THIS IN THE BIKE SHED.

ER, SIR. THE CANTEEN'S RUN OUT OF FOOD AGAIN.

WHAT? I GAVE YOU FIVE POUNDS FOR MORE ONLY A MONTH AGO!

BILLS ARE GOING THROUGH THE ROOF THESE DAYS.

SO I SEE, SIR!

TWIRL

CLICK

SCHOOL SAFE

OH, NO! THE LAST OF THE PETTY CASH HAS JUST RUN OUT!

OH, DEAR! THIS IS A BLACK DAY FOR BASH STREET SCHOOL.

ONE BLACK DAY COMIN' UP.

SCHOOL SAFE

OPEN!

WHIRR!

PETTY CASH

SCUTTLE!

Olive breaks the bad news—

SO WE MAY HAVE TO SHUT DOWN THE SCHOOL DINNER HALL.

BUT WE WON'T GET OUR SCHOOL DINNERS.

WE CAN'T AFFORD TO DINE OUT.

SOB! WE'LL STARVE.

J. JONES BUTCHER

FILLET STEAK

PORK SAUSAGES

SLICED SAUSAGES

WE'LL NEVER TASTE A SIZZLING SAUSAGE AGAIN.

ASSORTED VEGETABLES

WE'LL HAVE TO GROW OUR OWN.

CAN'T GROW JAM ROLY POLY 'N' CUSTARD THOUGH!

YOU LOT BELONG IN A ZOO!

SPLAT!

SPLOT!

HMM?!?

SO IN A ZOO WE WILL BE.

ZOO

BUT THIS IS BASH STREET SCHOOL!

BASH ST. SCHOOL

DUH! I'M CONFUSED.

COME ON! WE SHOULD FIND ALL WE NEED IN HERE.

SCHOOL DRAMA CLUB STORES

EH? IT'S A FOOD STORE I WANT.

Soon —

IT'S COMING ON GREAT. WHERE DID ALL THIS WOOD COME FROM?

ER, DON'T ASK!

THUD

THAT WOULD BE TELLING!

BAM

HELP! SOME LOWLIFE'S NICKED MY LADDER!

DOUGAL GLAZING THE WINDOW CLEANER

Back at the zoo —

ROLL UP! ROLL UP! VISIT A ZOO LIKE NO OTHER.

ZOO

TOSS

ADMISSION 50p

HERE WE HAVE OUR PAIR OF ELEPHANTS. THIS IS RAJAH, OUR INDIAN ONE.

ER, EXCUSE ME! THERE'S ONLY ONE ELEPHANT HERE.

THIS IS OUR MONKEY HOUSE!

BUT THERE'S JUST A SINGLE GORILLA — A WOODEN ONE AT THAT.

NO! AS YOU CAN NOW SEE, IT'S A MONKEY HOUSE ALRIGHT.

WOW! QUITE A MONKEY PUZZLE!

OPEN

OO-OO-OO!

CHORTLE! THEY DO LIKE SHINY OBJECTS, SIR. CLEVER CHIMP'S TALKING TO YOUR FALSE TEETH.

CHATTER CHATTER

SCLOOP!

CHATTER! CHATTER!

HISS!

RAASP!

WHEEE!

AAIEE!!

AHEM! AS YOU PROBABLY KNOW, THE WHALE POPULATION IS RAPIDLY SHRINKING.

GOSH!

HISS!

Inevitably—

GRR! THIS ZOO'S A TOTAL FAKE.

WE WANT OUR MONEY BACK!

I'VE SEEN MORE ANIMALS PLAYING FOR BEANOTOWN UNITED.

OO-ER!

JUST WAIT TILL YOU SEE THE CREATURE THAT AWAITS YOU OVER HERE.

HMPH! THIS BETTER BE GOOD.

YEAH!

GOT TO HIDE!

DIVE

DIVE

CAN'T BEAR TO LOOK.

DIVE

BURY!

BURY!

CHUCKLE! IT'S USUALLY THE OSTRICH WHO BURIES HIS HEAD IN THE SAND.

In Head's study —

SHOULD BE ENOUGH MONEY THERE TO SAVE OUR SCHOOL DINNERS.

ZOO

Minutes later —

HUH? NOBODY NICKS NUTHIN' OFFA ME!

SNAFFLE

WOT'S YOUR GAME, MUSH? THAT'S MY BIKER JACKET.

SSH! THAT'S LEMMY, OUR LEATHERBACK TURTLE YOU'RE SHOUTING AT.

PAT! PAT! PAT! PAT!

ZOO

MEET PLUG THE OSTRICH!

AAGH!

FLAP!

FLAP!

ZOO

IT'S 'ORRIBLE!

AND SO REAL, IT'S UNREAL!

I SAY! SPLENDID WORK, YOUNG DANNY!

Later, in the dining hall —

THIS IS FOR ALL YOU HUNGRY ZOO ANIMALS . . .

SLURP! BRING ON OUR SCRUMMY TUCK.

YUMSIE!

# THE BASH STREET KIDS in TOMB FOOLERY

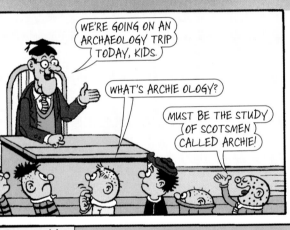

WE'RE GOING ON AN ARCHAEOLOGY TRIP TODAY, KIDS.

WHAT'S ARCHIE OLOGY?

MUST BE THE STUDY OF SCOTSMEN CALLED ARCHIE!

ARCHAEOLOGY IS THE STUDY OF OLD HISTORICAL RELICS.

STAFF ROOM

PLENTY OF THEM IN THERE TO STUDY, SIR!

YEAH! FOSSILS AND DINOSAURS!

One school bus trip later —

OH, I FORGOT TO MENTION — THE TRIP IS TO ANCIENT EGYPT.

WOW! MUST PHONE MY MUMMY!

BEANOTOWN AIRPORT

EGYPT! THAT'S EVEN FURTHER THAN DUNDEE.

Bus

In the airport terminal —

COME OFF OF THERE. WE'VE GOT TO GO THROUGH THE SECURITY CHECK NOW.

SECURITY

CAROUSEL

ANYBODY FOR A QUICK GAME OF FOOTY?

YEAH! IT'LL CALM OUR PRE-FLIGHT NERVES.

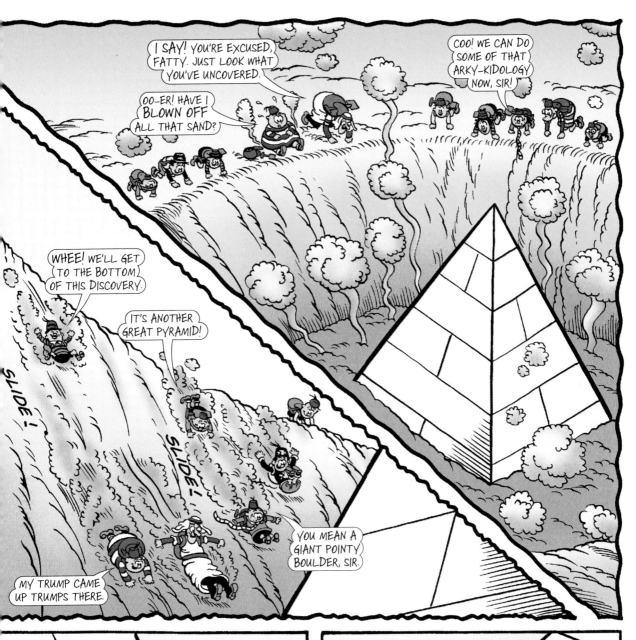

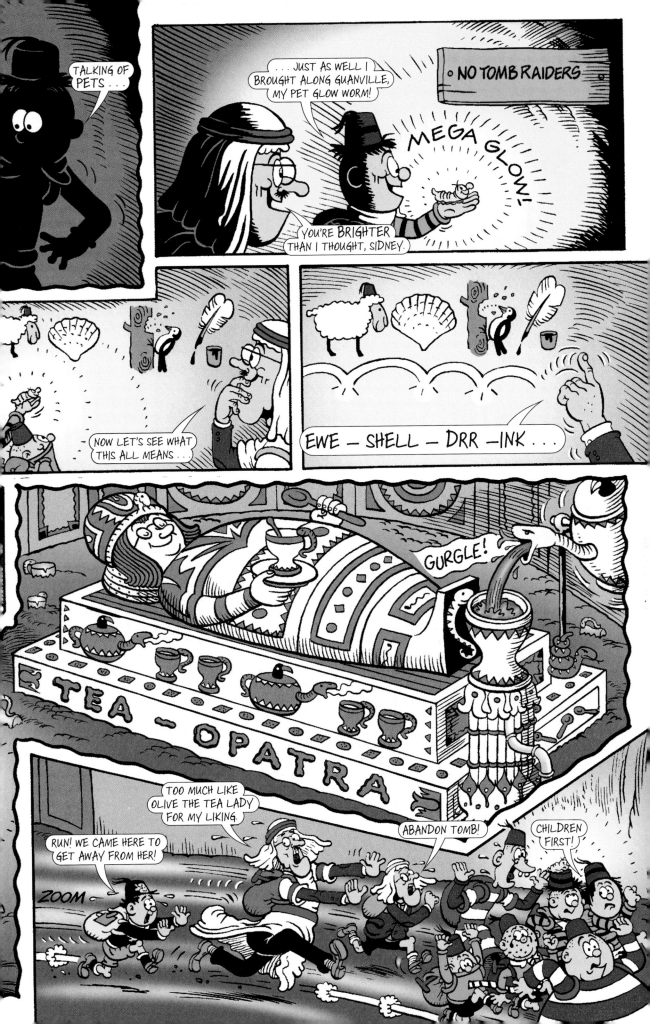

GRIMEWATCH UK

GOOD EVENING! WE'VE HAD REPORTS OF AN ATTEMPTED BREAK-IN AT BASH STREET SCHOOL. YES, THAT'S BREAK-IN, NOT BREAK-OUT!

ON AIR

At the scene —

THESE DEEP FOOTPRINTS AND THE IMPRINT OF A GRIMY FACE COVERED IN CHOCOLATE ARE THE ONLY CLUES.

WHIRR!

POLICE FORENSIC EXPERTS WERE SOON ON THE SCENE AND THEY THINK THEY MAY HAVE COME UP WITH SOMETHING.

POLICE TENT

THE BRILLIANT BEANO ARTIST, MR DAVID SUTHERLAND, HAS BEEN HELPING TO TRY TO IMPROVE THE SMUDGED FACE.

AYE! IT CERTAINLY NEEDS IMPROVING.

SOME VIEWERS MAY FIND THE FOLLOWING IMAGE DISTURBING.

CHEAP ART BOARD

IF YOU THINK YOU KNOW THIS GRUBBY CHARACTER, GIVE US A CALL.

GRIMEWATCH WILL BE BACK ON-AIR LATER IN THE BOOK.

DS

Soon —

I NEED A NEW CHAIR!

YES, SIR!

Shortly —

I DIDN'T HAVE A NEW ONE — SO I'VE FIXED YOUR OLD CHAIR.

ER ... IT'S A BIT HIGH, JANITOR!

Then —

HE'S FAINTED!

F-A-I-N-T!

DOH!

THUD!

THE ONLY WAY TO CURE YOUR FEAR OF HEIGHTS — IS TO FACE THE PROBLEM.

OOOOH!

MY UNCLE CAN HELP. THE ONE WHO CAN FLY.

At the airfield —

HOW MUCH WILL THE FLIGHT COST?

A ROLL OF STICKY TAPE AND SOME CARDBOARD!

TAKE OFF IN FIVE MINUTES ...

GASP!

... ONCE I'VE MADE A FEW MINOR REPAIRS! HMM!

COUGH!

PHUT! PHUT!

SPLUTTER!

URR-OOO-CM!

THINK IT'LL WORK?

WILL TEACHER BE CURED OF HIS FEAR OF HEIGHTS?

GRR! NO!

EH?

HE NEVER GOT OFF THE GROUND!

GNASH! GNASH!

SNARL! C'MERE!

DOINK!

'ULP! NOW WE HAVE A FEAR — OF TEACHER CATCHING US!

AAARGH!

LEAP

CRASH!

LUNCHTIME, SIR! HAR-HAR!

In the dining hall.

AH! WHAT I'D GIVE TO WIN ONE TROPHY!

BAH!

HOI! STOP PLAYING WITH YOUR FOOD!

WELL WE'RE CERTAINLY NOT GOING TO EAT IT! LOOK WHAT I'VE MADE!

HMM!

MOULD

STIR

SEE! CHOMP! MUNCH!

DON'T EAT! I'VE JUST HAD A GREAT IDEA!

PUSH

I'M GOING TO ENTER THESE FOR A SCHOOL'S ART COMPETITION!

HA-HA-HA!

TRUNDLE

HMM!

THEY'RE SO UNUSUAL — WE'LL WIN!

JUDGE

THE JUDGE CHANGED HIS MIND! WE'VE WON FIRST PRIZE, SIR!

EH? WOW! HE DID?

TURN

Later —

TROPHY CABINET

DAY OUT ON ME! MY TREAT!

WAHEY!

HA-HA! THE KIDS FOOLED THE TEACHER AGAIN! THEY DIDN'T WIN ANY PRIZE! THEY MADE THIS ONE OUT OF DOUGH! I'LL HAVE EATEN IT BY THE TIME THEY RETURN FROM THE PIZZA PLACE! MUNCH! CHOMP! GUZZLE!

OFF WE GO, KIDS!

1st PRIZE

I WOULDN'T GIVE TUP-
PENCE FOR DANNY'S
CHANCES OF ARRIVING ON
TIME ON THAT THING.

PLUG'S TAKING THE PLUNGE IN A DUGOUT CANOE,
CHISELLED WITH HIS OWN TEETH, NO LESS.

# GET ME TO SCHOOL ON TIME

FOR ONCE, FATTY'S NOT THE ONE CALLED JUMBO.
HE'S MORE USED TO HANDLING A JUMBO SAUSAGE
THAN AN ELEPHANT.

SYDNEY HOPES TO SHAVE A FEW MINUTES OFF HIS FASTEST TIME TO SCHOOL WITH HIS CUTTING EDGE ROLLER BLADES!

'ERBERT'S NOT MUCH CHANCE OF STAYING ON COURSE IF HIS DOG TEAM SPOT WINSTON THE CAT!

SPOTTY DOESN'T KNOW IF HE'S COMING OR GOING THIS MORNING. AT LEAST HE CAN SEE WHERE HE'S BEEN.

WATCH YOU DON'T RUN OVER THAT HEDGE-HOG, TOOTS, OR YOU MAY BOUNCE HIGHER THAN YOU'D LIKE.

**HEADMASTER MAGIC**

In class IIB.

BLAH! BLAH! BLAH!

Do not disturb

ZZZZZ!

Suddenly —

WOW!

WHUMP

FLASH

I SIT MY EXAM TO JOIN THE MAGIC CIRCLE TODAY CAN I TRY OUT SOME TRICKS?

HEH! O...

YOU WILL ACT LIKE A CHICKEN ... CHICKEN ...

SWING SWING

HO-HO!

WAA! DOWN, CHICKEN!

PECK! PECK! PECK

HO-HO! NOT MUCH OF A TRICK — SMIFFY OFTEN THINKS HE'S A CHICKEN ...

SMASH!

... OR A GOAT ...

... OR A DESK! HA-HA!

NEVER MIND, SIR. I BET IF WE ALL WENT INTO THAT CUPBOARD — YOU COULD MAKE US DISAPPEAR!

ER ... WELL!

CUP- BOARD

YES ... I'LL MAKE YOU ALL DISAPPEAR IN A FLASH!

ABERA ... CA ... DOOBRA!

SLAM SHUT

CUP- BOARD

WAVE

FIRST OF ALL I NEED A VOLUNTEER!

PSST! HANDS DOWN, KIDS!

HO-HO! SMIFFY ALWAYS GETS IT WRONG!

OKAY, DANNY!

AHA! A VOLUNTEER!

PROD!

UP

YOU ARE SLEEPY . . . SLEEPY . . .

GNAH! DOO! BLOO!

SWING

K A CARD. NY CARD.

HMM!

YOU'VE MISSED THE PACK!

GRAB

NO . . . DON'T PULL THAT!

HA-HA! THAT FLOWER ON A STRING HAS SET OFF ALL OF THE HEAD'S TRICKS!

BOYLP!

NO . . . MY MAGIC!

PYOING

COO!

OPEN

TA-RA!

'ULP! YOU'VE DONE IT!

ER . . . I CAN'T GET THEM BACK! OO . . . ER! ABERA . . . CA . . . HO . . . HUM!

VWSH

FRANTIC WAVING

GASP! WHAT'LL WE TELL THEIR PARENTS? OR EVEN OLIVE? WE'LL HAVE TO EAT THE SCHOOL LUNCHES OURSELVES!

HA-HA! WE LEFT BY OUR SECRET ESCAPE TUNNEL WHICH COMES OUT HERE.

HO-HO!

HA-HA! WE'LL TAKE THE REST OF THE DAY OFF!

LIFT

LIFT

DROP

LIFT

JANITOR'S VEGETABLE PATCH

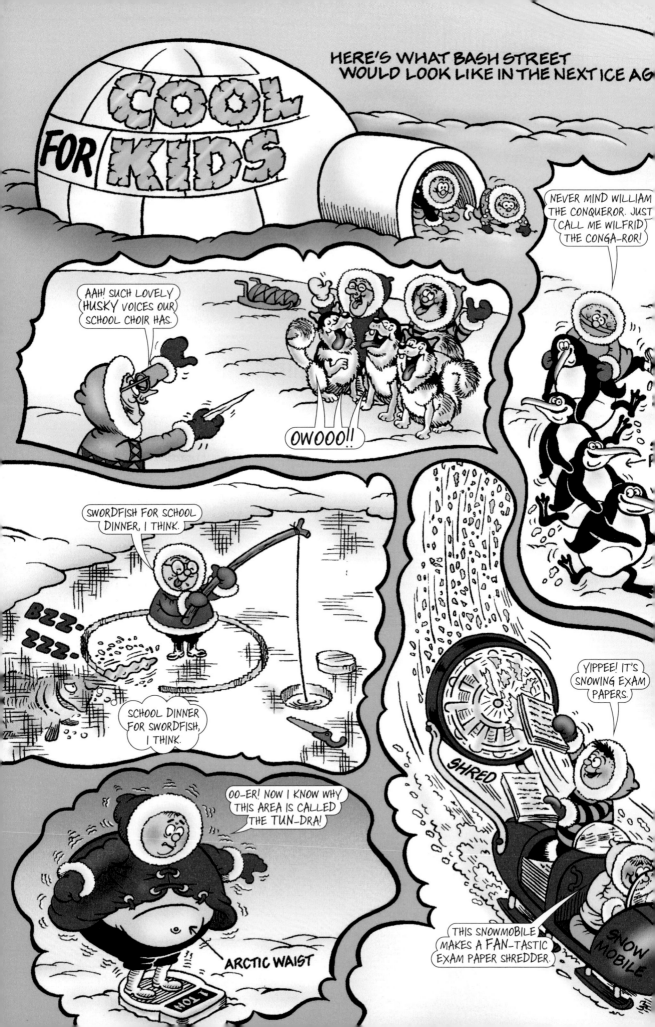

PUP PARADE *with the BASH ST. PUPS*

BONES  PEEPS  'ENRY  SNIFFY  TUBBY  SPOTTY  MANFRID  WIGGY  PUG

What's daft Sniffy up to?

DIVE

EEK!

WAHEY!

SPLOSH!

HUH!

THUD!

GURR!

But...

THEN—

Why is he now putting his nose through the fence?

ON THE OTHER SIDE—

SPLASH!

SPLOF!

Tum...tee... tum...

WHITE PAINT

Great! I feel better now!

EH? Better with a white nose?

LAUGH BREEDS
SCOTTISH DEERHOUND

No, no, Bones! I'm much healthier! Didn't you know that a dog with a wet nose is healthy?

Haw-haw! So that's what he's been doing!

Grimewatch will be back on-air later in the book.

AN EARTHQUAKE! TAKE COVER!

NOT A QUAKE, SIR!

TREMBLE

ONLY FATTY FAINTING WHEN HE HEARD ABOUT THE 'NO EATING IN CLASS' RULE. HA-HA!

GASP! HE EVEN EATS WHILE FAINTING!

CHOMP! MUNCH!

WELL, NO MORE EATING AS FROM NOW!

HUH! WE DON'T EAT OFTEN IN CLASS, ANYWAY.

YES . . .

. . . GIVE ME ALL OF YOUR FOOD! THAT'S AN ORDER!

MENU

DOH! IT WASN'T A BAD DREAM!

IN HERE WITH IT!

BOO!

SWEEP

PSST! I HAVE AN IDEA. LET'S SNEAK OUT!

HOW CAN WE SNEAK OUT, DANNY?

CAN WE START READING OUR BOOKS, SIR? WE DON'T WANT TO WASTE ANY MORE TIME.

NNNGH!

WOBBLE

WOW! SO KEEN! WHAT A CHANGE ONCE THEY PUT EATING OUT OF THEIR MINDS.

. . . AND TURN TO PAGE . . .

HA-HA! WE HAVEN'T GIVEN UP EATING — WE MADE BOOKS, PENCILS AND ERASERS FROM THE KITCHEN SUPPLY OF MARZIPAN!

GUZZLE CHOMP

CHOMP CHEW

CHEW

DON'T YOU THINK TO PULL THE BLIND DOWN?

TUG!

ER . . . NO!

THERE! WHY COULDN'T YOU HAVE DONE THAT?

GIANT TUG

BECAUSE . . .

Suddenly.

WHIRRRRRRR

WAAAA!

. . . THE SPRING'S TOO STRONG ON IT! HO-HO!

SMIRK

TUMBLE

EEK! THE WINDOW'S OPEN! AAA!

BOUNCE

WOW!

ROLL

YIKES!

FLATTEN

SPIN

OKAY, NOW? THEN I SHALL BEGIN AGAIN WITH A MATHS LESSON!

. . . BLAH . . . SEVEN PLUS . . . BLAH . . .

LET'S GO!

HA-HA! WE USED FLOORBOARDS TO BLOCK UP THE WINDOW!

TOO DIM LIGHT NOW FOR TEACHER TO SEE WE'VE GONE!

YAHOO!

FREE!

DIG

WE MUST GET RID OF THINGS WE HAVE NO USE FOR.

NO CHANCE OF NEEDING THIS!

SIGH! TRUE!

NNGH! WHAT'S IN HERE?

NO! DON'T OPEN THAT!

AAARGH!

THROW

WOW! EEK!

DUST NOW, KIDS!

CHORTLE!

DUST

AATISHOOO!

WAA!

AATISHOOO!

OO . . . ER!

RUMBLE!

WHEE!

AHA! THIS IS MORE LIKE IT! BUT WE HAVE THROWN SOMETHING OUT IN OUR 'SPRING CLEAN'.

EH?

THE HEAD'S NOTE! TITTER!

YAHOO!

HEH-HEH!

FOR LAUGHS

JELLY BABIES

FIND OUT WHO'S GUILTY
ON PAGES 86 AND 87

EDITED HIGH-LIGHTS

IT'S TIME TO PRODUCE ANOTHER EDITION OF THE SCHOOL MAGAZINE. I'M THE EDITOR.

YOU CAN BE CHIEF PHOTOGRAPHER.

I'VE BEEN FRAMED. GLUMPH!

SPLAT TWANG

PUSH

HUH! I WANTED TO BE THE EDITOR.

THE REST OF YOU ARE N REPORTERS. NOW BUZZ AND FIND SOME STORIE

FOLLOW ME, NEWSHOUNDS

LOOK! ALL OF OUR SCHOOL TROPHIES HAVE BEEN PINCHED!

WAIT! DON'T WASTE YOUR FILM.

TROPHY CABINET

ALL WE'VE EVER WON ARE WOODEN SPOONS! HERE THEY ARE.

I'LL NOT BOTHER.

LOOK! THE HEAD'S PLAYING GOLF IN SCHOOL TIME.

WE'LL PUT THAT ON THE SPORTS PAGE.

CRASH

THWACK

In the kitchen.

OLIVE'S MAKING BISCUITS.

CLICK

ROLL

WHAT WE REALLY NEED TO SELL THE MAGAZINE IS A FREE GIFT — BUT WHAT?

IIB MAG

II MAG

So —

OLIVE'S GIVEN US HER BISCUITS TO USE AS FREE GIFTS.

THEY'RE ROCK HARD! CAN'T EAT THEM!

BUT THEY MAKE GREAT SOLES FOR YOUR BOOTS!

WE'RE PLAYING TIDDLYWINKS WITH THEM!

STICK

GLUE

CLICK

CLICK

EXTRA! EXTRA! READ ALL ABOUT IT!

WE'RE SELLING RE NUMBERS OF O MAGAZINE.

BASH ST. SCHOC

HAHA!

IIB MAG

II MA

II MA

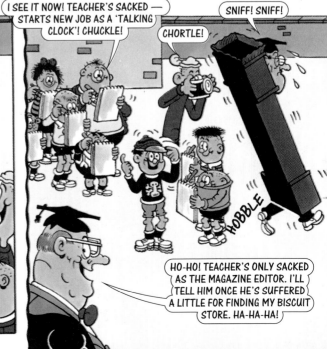

# WHAT GOES ON BEHIND THE BIKE SHED

BEHIND THE BIKE SHED'S A GREAT PLACE TO PRACTISE OUR GRAFFITI!

THIS BEATS ART CLASS.

skule stinks    spelying shud B band

SPLUTTER! THIS IS OUTRAGEOUS. IN FACT, IT'S AN OUTRAGE!

ERM, WASN'T US, SIR.

IT WAS HIM!

skule stinks    spelying shud B

CUTHBERT! - NOT YOU OF ALL PUPILS!

S-SORRY, SIR. I SIMPLY COULDN'T HELP MYSELF.

d B band    I LIKE TEACHER SCHOOL IS SPLENDID MORE HOMEWORK PLEASE    FOR SIR

Much elbow grease later —

PHEW! IT WON'T COME OFF, SIR.

GASP! YOU'LL JUST HAVE TO LIVE WITH OUR ART, SIR.

SCRUB! SCRUB!

SCRUB!

HMPH! WE SHALL SEE.

SWING    CHUG    BUILDING SITE

CACKLE! THERE - I'VE RUBBED IT OUT GOOD AND PROPER.

**BLAM**

SWING    WHEE    ZOOM

GLOOP! OUR LOVELY BIKE SHED!

EEK!

PONK

GOLLY GOSH!

GRIMEWATCH UK

GOOD EVENING, VIEWERS. YOU JOIN US AT A VITAL STAGE OF THIS INVESTIGATION.

TUCK SHOP

HEAVY FOOTSTEPS

WHIRR!

SLURP! WINDOWS MADE OF TOFFEE. I CAN LICK MY WAY IN.

LICK! LICK!

HAPPY BIRTHDAY

MADE IT! WHAT A PIECE OF CAKE!

LEAP

YOU IS NICKED!

CRASH!

BURST!

ER, EXCUSE ME! I'M NICK!

WHIRR!

AAGH!

MIKE

BAH! I'LL HAVE TO MAKE FATTY ANOTHER SURPRISE BIRTHDAY CAKE NOW.

OO-ER!

WHIRR!

YOU CAN ALL SLEEP SOUNDLY NOW, VIEWERS. FATTY'S SAFELY BEHIND BARS!

CHOMP! YEAH — CHOCCY BARS. THEY'LL DO TILL I GET MY CAKE!

GUZZLE! GNASH!

WHIRR

MIKE

CHOC BARS

DS

# MOTLEY CREW

SIR! LOOK, AN ALIEN!

HA-HA! IT'S ONLY . . .

SIR! SIR! AN ALIEN . . . COME AND SEE!

ER . . . OH!

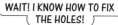

WAIT! I KNOW HOW TO FIX THE HOLES!

Back at school.

WE HAVE A ROWING BOAT IN HERE.

BUT IT'S FULL OF HOLES, SIR!

PERFEC...

CUSTARD

. . . GO!

BANG!

YAHOO! GO FOR IT!

PONK!

RUDDER

A few minutes later.

SPLASH SPLASH SPLASH

SIGH! I DIDN'T REALLY THINK WE STOOD A CHANCE.

Then —

EH?

HUP ... ONE ... TWO!

SPLASH

... POSH STREET SCHOOL'S BOATING TEAM! HA-HA!

HUMPH!

WAA!

GLUB!

HAR-HAR!

SPLASH

SPLASH

HAW-HAW! WHY NOT GIVE US A RACE?

YES ... GOOD IDEA! WE HAVE A BOAT!

VERY STRONG! OLIVE'S PANCAKES AS PATCHES AND HER CUSTARD AS GLUE!

GET OFF, FATTY!

WE'RE READY FOR THE POSH STREET TEAM!

POSH STREET TEACHER

GET READY ... SET ...

FIZZZ

BAH!

WE'VE WON!

YAHOO!

WINNING POST

BUMP!

BOO-HOO! BEATEN BY ... BASH STREET SCHOOL!

SOB!

BOO! HOO!

SPLASH!

SPLASH!

WELL DONE!

YES! ALL DUE TO OLIVE'S PANCAKES!

THEY FELL OFF HALFWAY ALONG THE COURSE — WE HAD TO RUN ALONG THE RIVERBED TO THE FINISH! HA-HA!

HO-HO! I SUPPOSE WE CHEATED BUT — IT WAS GREAT TO SEE THE POSH STREET PUPILS' FACES!

# A GALE FARCE WIND

HO-HO! IT'S GALE FORCE WINDS TO... I'M THE ONLY THING IN BEANOTO... WHICH WON'T BLOW AWAY!

WE MUST KEEP HOLD OF HIM!

Reader's voice.

YOU'RE VERY POPULAR TODAY, FATTY!

GRRR! MY CAR!

SCHOOL

BLAST

SWOOSH

SWING

I'LL FIX THEM!

WHIRR

TUG

AHA! GOT IT!

WHIRR

INTO CLASS... THERE'S WO... TO BE DON...

BOP

GUST OF W...

GOOD! I NEED T... SKIN FOR LUN... TIME!

SPREAD

YUM! I CAN ALMOST TASTE THAT JACKET NOW!

ON THE COUNT OF THREE, PALS! READY!

...AND IN 1718...

...3...2...1... PULL!

POP
POP
TUG
POP
POP
TUG
POP

SWOOS!

# A CLASS IIB AVOIDED

CLASS IIB

WE'LL LOOK IN ON THEM NOW!

CLASS IIB

ER . . . HELLO, YOUR HEADSHIP!

EEK!

CHOM

I'M OFF!

OH!

But —

HAR-HAR!

MOST INTERESTING!

HEH-HEH!

HUH! WE'RE ALL OUT OF FRUIT!

WE'VE HAD ENOUGH OF THIS. LET'S GO!

RUN FOR IT!

YAHOO!

TRAMPLE

STOMP

AHA!

HANDY THINGS BOOMERANGS!

WHIRRRR

WHAT'S THAT?

THROW

TUG

ERK?

WOW!

# PUP PARADE

with the BASH St. PUPS

BONES  PEEPS  'ENRY  SNIFFY  TUBBY  SPOTTY  MANFRID  WIGGY  PUG

MAN WITH HANDCART OF SEAFOOD PASSING THE BIN.

BUMP!  DONK!

Har-har! Wonder who I can nip in this bin?

LEAP!
NIP!
NIP!

Har-har!  YEOWL!

If we had an empty shell—the type you can hear the sea in, we could trap that naughty crab!

Huh! We don't have a shell.

DAFT SNIFFY.

But we do have an empty head!

Some water in here to make a 'sea' noise.

SPLOSH! GURGLE!

That tickles, Bones!

It's worked!

Is that the sea I hear?

Got him!

Who?

PLUG
STUFF
SPLASH!  SPLOSH!

The crab's out of the way, but it's made Sniffy act even dafter than usual! Ho-ho-ho!

Oh!.. I do like to be beside the seaside...

SIDEWAYS SWERVE

SNAP!

CLICK!

## LAUGH BREEDS
### MINIATURE BULL TERRIER